Cheer up, it's Lent!

Cheer up, it's Lent!

A LENT BOOK
FOR THE WHOLE FAMILY

TONY CASTLE

kevin
mayhew

First published in 2003 by

KEVIN MAYHEW LTD
Buxhall, Stowmarket, Suffolk, IP14 3BW
E-mail: info@kevinmayhewltd.com

KINGSGATE PUBLISHING INC
1000 Pannell Street, Suite G, Columbia, MO 65201
E-mail: sales@kingsgatepublishing.com

9 8 7 6 5 4 3 2 1 0

ISBN 1 84417 167 1
Catalogue No 1500657

Cover design by Jonathan Stroulger
Edited by Katherine Laidler
Typesetting by Louise Selfe
Printed and bound in Great Britain

for Angela and Simon as they begin life together

Contents

Introduction

Cheer up, it's Lent, and we have Easter, the great feast of the Lord's Resurrection, in our sights. Whether we are giving up, taking up or making up, let's do it the Jesus way – with a smile. He gave special instructions to his friends (Matthew 6:16) not to be long-faced and miserable when they were giving up food and being sorry for their misdemeanours. If the adults in a family go into Lent with a long face, you can be sure the children will follow suit. If something is worth doing, it's worth doing cheerfully. Didn't St Paul say, 'God loves a cheerful giver'? (2 Corinthians 9:7)

The word 'family' in the subtitle of this book is a bit of problem. Each family on planet earth is uniquely different from every other family. We believe and accept that each individual is uniquely different from every other individual, so obviously when you put together a group of unique individuals you get a family that is distinctively different from every other family. Strangely, this is not always acknowledged. Additionally, by 'family' are we thinking of a young family with pre-school under-fives, or a mix which will include the odd teenager? Or are all the younger members of the family of secondary school age? Difficulties abound. In offering some material for Lent, the best one can do is to hope that something in these pages will strike a chord, appeal as useful, and seem practical in your particular family.

McDonald's takeaways, home-delivered pizzas, microwave ready-meals all lead to trays in front of the telly and away from sitting down, as a family, to a shared meal. Many mourn the passing of the traditional evening meal – whatever you name it – tea, dinner or supper. However, there are a growing number who try to retain the family-together meal with its unity-building values.

For many families the only time they are together, during the week, is when they eat together. In the 1950s the Christian slogan was 'the family that prays together stays together'. There might be as much truth, 50 years later, in 'the family that eats together has more hope of staying together'.

If Lent is to happen at all in the Christian family, as a shared experience, it has its best hope for success at the family meal. **Table time** together can, with a little organisation and a determination to make it work, transform Lent into a true preparation for Easter for all the family. Lent only has meaning as a preparation for Easter. It originated out of the community's need to prepare its new recruits for baptism and reception into the Christian family at Easter.

Jesus, the teacher, was the greatest storyteller of all time. He used stories most efficiently and storytelling remains one of the best teaching tools. That's why, every day of the 40, there is a **table tale.**

Jesus also made great and regular use of **table talk.** The Gospels continually have Jesus sharing a meal and using a table ministry, with all manner of people.

The material is structured around the traditional 40 days of Lent, although – and this needs emphasising – the material does not have to be used in the order in which it is offered.

The Bible seems to show that God considers 40 days a spiritually significant period of preparation. Noah was prepared for the new beginning by 40 days of rain. Moses spent 40 days of preparation for his role as leader on Mount Sinai. Elijah travelled on his God-given journey of 40 days after one special meal. Under Jonah's eye the city of Nineveh was transformed over a period of 40 days. Jesus spent 40 days of preparation for his ministry in the desert. It took 40 days from the resurrection before the Apostles were prepared sufficiently for action after the Lord's ascension.

It is not likely that any family will be able to use all the material; there are sure to be days when it is not practical either to eat together or to apply the material. Because of the wide interpretation possible for the word 'family' some of the material is not suitable for a family with young children; some 'days' are more suitable for teenagers. Whoever is going to lead the **table time** needs to select what is suitable.

Either at the beginning of the family meal or, if more convenient, at the end an adult or young person can lead the **table time**, an introduction to the theme; read or, better still, tell the **table tale** and conclude with **table talk**, which is not intended to be read but to be a stimulus to conversation about the story, leading into a relevant prayer, **God talk.** It's an attempt to balance talking to one another and talking to God.

One of the most important marks of the Christian is joy. If we are going to make an effort this Lent, let's do it cheerfully.

1
Give up (1)

Table time

Lent begins with ashes, and ashes suggest fire. To get ashes something has been burnt. Last year, on Palm Sunday, we were given a palm cross each *(you may have one from last year to show)*. The church gets the ashes from burning the palms that are left over. Lots of people will be talking today, the beginning of Lent, about what they are going to give up for Lent. Are we going to give up something? What's the point of bothering?

Table tale

The teacher told the class that it was the beginning of Lent. Lent, she explained, was a very old English word for Spring.

'Julie, what are you going to give up for Lent?'

'I'm going to give up school,' Julie replied cheekily, and all the class laughed.

Jack called out, 'I'm giving up homework.' More laughter.

'That's a good idea,' replied the teacher. 'I'll give up running the lunch time club.'

'You can't do that,' Julie called out. 'We all like going to that.'

'Nor can you give up school,' said the teacher. 'Now let's think about something sensible to give up for Lent.'

Table talk

Before we say any more about giving up, let's think for a moment about why. What's the point of it? First, we don't want to do something just because other people are doing it; we must have a good reason, otherwise it has no value. Lent's a kind of journey. Over 40 days we are travelling towards the great, important feast of Easter. If you are walking a long distance you have to be fit and you can't carry much luggage. So during Lent we try to shed some of the unnecessary baggage that we carry, some of the bad habits. Let's talk about that.

God talk

God is present with us here
and has heard everything we have shared in the last few minutes.
Dear Lord,
help us to make the next few weeks very special.
Help us to prepare well for the great feast of Easter.
Please be with us in all the things we do
and the resolutions that we make.
Amen.

2
Give up (2)

Table time

Last time we talked about *why* it's a good idea to give up something for Lent. At the time of Jesus the Jewish people used to sacrifice – that is 'give up' to God – something that was precious to them, or use their money to buy something that could be offered to God on the altar in the Temple. They tried to give the best they had, not some rubbishy thing that they didn't want any more. So 'giving up' is supposed to be hard, not easy. There's a famous story in the Bible we can remind ourselves about.

Table tale

Abraham, who lived nearly 2000 years before Jesus was born, had found a faith in God and was very keen to do whatever God asked. He and his wife Sarah had wanted a baby for many years and at last, when they were no longer young, they had a son; they called him Isaac. Now, at that time, all of the tribes that lived around Canaan, where Abraham and Sarah lived, believed in many gods and some offered men, women or children as sacrifices to these gods. They offered, or gave up, human beings to their gods! When Isaac was about 12, Abraham was very surprised when God, his God, asked him to give up, in sacrifice, his own much-loved son. He took the boy, who did not know what was happening, to a hill called Moriah. Abraham got Isaac to carry the wood for the fire up the hill. When they got to the top Abraham built an altar; then he tied up Isaac and laid him on the wood, on top of the altar. Abraham was just about to kill his son when God stopped him. 'Abraham,' the voice said, 'do not harm the boy.' Abraham had proved his love and his trust in God. Abraham and Isaac together gave up a ram in sacrifice instead.
Genesis 22:1-13

Table talk

Now that story comes from a very long time ago, when life was very different, but the message doesn't change. Abraham loved God so much that he was prepared to give the most wonderful thing he had, his son. So if we are going to give up or offer up something to God this Lent, it's got to be something really worthwhile. It's insulting to God to play around at it. If I'm going to give up chocolate for Lent – and that's a popular one, these days – that's fine, but I must do it wholeheartedly and properly. Let's talk about what, realistically, we can do.

God talk

Loving Father,
you don't ask us to do anything for Lent,
but you do want us to show our love for you.
If we are going to give up something for Lent,
please help us to do it cheerfully and generously,
as a gift of love to you.
Amen.

3

Give up (3)

Table time

Schools have testing times. We all know that. It's called assessment, and the idea is that learning stops for a very short break, while the teacher finds out if the pupils have learnt anything! It's silly to carry on if the children haven't understood and learnt what they were taught. The same thing happens at places of work, for adults. The work we do is assessed and the people in charge decide if we are working properly.

If we want to be good friends of Jesus we have to stop sometimes and ask ourselves: are we really doing the things Jesus wants us to? We don't take a test, but we do need to assess how things are going. That's another reason for Lent: a chance to look at how we are living our lives as friends of Jesus. We might have to give up some bad habit, unkind action or thoughtless behaviour.

Table tale

Jamie was 20 months old. Because he could walk and talk he thought that he was much too big to be put in a high chair. But Jamie had a 4-year-old brother, who made a terrible mess when he ate at the table, and he had a sister of 4 months. His mum had to put Jamie in the high chair so that she could cope with the other two. Jamie screamed and shouted and kept trying to stand up in the high chair. His mum would get him sitting down, and then he would stand up again. And this was repeated again and again. His mum was trying hard to be patient and cope. At last she put reins on him and really tied him down. Jamie screamed and said, 'I'm still standing up, inside.'

Table talk

We all want to be free and do our own thing. And, as you've just heard, it starts very early in life. What Jamie was not old enough to understand was that we have to respect and, when we can, help other people. Jamie was only in the high chair because his mother could not manage things any other way. Jamie was obstinate and he was making everything worse – especially for his mother who loved him. We have to think about our actions. Are we being obstinate, wanting our own way without any respect for anyone else? We need, each of us, to examine and assess how we behave, and ask if we could not be more loving and considerate.

God talk

Loving Father,
you know us better than we know ourselves.
You know every thought that we have –
and every temptation.
Help us to use Lent to look at our behaviour
and see if we can be less full of ourselves
and more full of you and your love.
Amen.

4
Take up (1)

Table time

Last time we talked about giving up; in other words, going without something. That was a way that we can say 'no' to ourselves. How about saying 'yes'? Now that Lent has got going, should we think about doing something extra, not just giving up? Jesus' friend and cousin, John, who baptised people, was big on giving up. 'Give up bullying people,' he told the soldiers. 'Give up taking extra money off people,' he told the tax collectors.

All that was good, of course, but Jesus comes along and he is much more positive. He says, 'Take up your cross and follow me.' Can we take on or take up something extra?

Table tale

The three children were slumped in front of the telly watching the latest episode of their favourite soap, when Mum popped her head in and said, 'Mrs Collins is at the door. She's going on holiday for two weeks. Would anyone go in her house every day to feed her cat?' Silence. 'Did you hear me?' Only the voices from the television could be heard.

'Helen, would you do it?' 'Can't,' she replied. 'Got too much homework.'

'How about you, Simon?' 'Sorry, too busy.'

'Would you do it, Michael?' 'No,' replied Michael, 'you know I hate cats.'

Helen suddenly had a change of heart. 'All right,' she said, 'I suppose I could do it.' 'Good,' said Mum, then her head disappeared from the doorway.

When Mrs Collins returned after her two week holiday she

was delighted that Helen had been in each day and not only fed the cat but also watered her plants. 'Here's a big bar of chocolate, a present from my holiday and £20 for being so generous and kind.'

As soon as Mrs Collins had gone the boys said, 'That's not fair.'

'Oh yes, it is,' retorted Mum. 'Each of you had the chance to take up the opportunity, and you didn't. Well done, Helen.'

Table talk

Lent gives us the opportunity of doing something extra, of taking up an activity that will show our love of God and perhaps help others too. What could we take up and do, to show our love of God and our love of others?

God talk

Loving God and Father,
you are not interested in celebrities or favourite TV programmes;
you are only interested in love.
And it's by love that you judge and evaluate people.
May our first interest be a love of you.
Help us to take up something that will help us to grow in your love.
May our second interest, as important as the first,
be the love of other people,
even if we find them hard to get on with.
Help us to take up something that will make both these loves
grow and develop.
Amen.

5
Take up (2)

Table time

Our theme is still 'taking up'. Last time we spoke of the words of Jesus, 'Take up your cross and follow me', but we did not examine them. We know that Jesus died on a wooden cross. We also know he had to carry that cross to the place where he was killed. It would have been very heavy and awkward to carry. Because he was so weak from the rough treatment he had received, he fell several times. Jesus did not choose to carry the cross; it was given to him, forced upon him and he had to accept it. When Jesus tells us to 'take up our cross' he is saying that he knows there are sometimes things in life that are forced upon us, conditions and circumstances that have not been chosen but have to be accepted.

Table tale

This poem has been around for a long time, but it still has a good message.

Today upon a bus I saw a girl with golden hair;
she seemed so gay, I envied her, and wish that I were half so fair;
I watched her as she rose to leave, and saw her hobble down the aisle.
She had one leg and wore a crutch, but as she passed – a smile.
Oh, God, forgive me when I whine;
I have two legs – the world is mine.

Later on I bought some sweets.
The boy who sold them had such charm, I thought I'd stop and talk awhile. If I were late, t'would do no harm.
And as we talked he said, 'Thank you, sir, you've really been so kind.
It's nice to talk to folks like you because, you see, I'm blind.'

19

Oh, God, forgive me when I whine;
I have two eyes – the world is mine.

Later, walking down the street, I met a boy with eyes so blue.
But he stood and watched the others play; it seemed he knew not
what to do.
I paused, and then I said, 'Why don't you join the others, dear?'
But he looked straight ahead without a word, and then I knew, he
couldn't hear.
Oh, God, forgive me when I whine;
I have two ears – the world is mine.

Two legs to take me where I go,
two eyes to see the sunset's glow,
two ears to hear all I should know,
Oh, God, forgive me when I whine;
I'm blest, indeed, the world is mine.
Tennyson Guyer

Table talk

There are some people in our world who have no sight, no hearing,
no speech or mobility; they have a cross to bear. There are men
and women who cannot find work and have big money problems.
There are children who are in families where there are very serious
problems; they have a cross to bear. We must always try to
improve things, but sometimes a person has just got to shoulder
their cross cheerfully and seek happiness in the best way that they
can. If we are free of a heavy cross to bear, we must thank God
and pray for strength for those who do have them to carry.

God talk

Thank you, Lord, for our family life.
Thank you for the good health that we enjoy
and for all your blessings that we take for granted.
We pray for those we know
who have a cross to bear in life,
and for the many that we don't know.
May they have the courage and the strength
to carry their crosses,
and may they be blessed with the cheerful support
of family and friends.
Amen.

6
Own up

Table time

Accidents, sadly, do happen and sometimes they happen because a person has misjudged something or made a simple mistake. Sometimes what has happened has been the deliberate action of a person or a group.

Table tale

The newspaper heading was 'Escape from the Incredible Hulk'. It looked as if Doreen Smalley's last moment had come when the incredible hulk dropped in. 'I was washing up at the sink, when I heard this low rumbling, and there was a trembling of the floor,' she said. 'I looked out of the window and couldn't believe my eyes. It looked like a great big tank coming across the front garden. It hit the house with a tremendous explosion of noise.'

In fact, it was a 12-foot-high, 20-ton runaway mechanical digger, which had been set on its way by a group of young vandals. They had by-passed the 'stop' devices with two bent nails.

Before demolishing the front of Mrs Smalley's house the digger had crossed three roads, demolished fencing and a lamp-post and written off three cars. Estimated damage, to the house alone, was set at £150,000.

West Yorkshire police were anxious to trace four boys between 9 and 12 who were seen running away from the council compound where the digger had been parked.

Table talk

A later newspaper report told how, when questioned, the boys said, 'It's not our fault. The compound was left unlocked!' Very often children and young people come out with 'It's not my fault', when it is obvious to everyone else that they are responsible; they did do it. Even when they are seen hurting someone or damaging something, out comes the excuse, 'It's not my fault'. One of the signs of growing up is being honest, owning up when we are responsible for something that has gone wrong. Before we can make up with one another – and with God – we have to be ready to own up.

God talk

God of all honesty and truth,
help us to own up
when we have done wrong,
so that any harm done
can be put right,
and we can try again.
Amen.

7

Make up (1)

Table time

We all know what make-up is. Actors use it when they are playing a part in a play. All the people we see on television, even the news presenters, have to put on make-up before they appear before the cameras. Women and girls use it to make themselves look beautiful. Sometimes it is used to cover up some skin blemish or mark.

Actors also put on make-up to help them as they pretend to be someone they are not; perhaps they are playing an old person or a bad person.

Jesus asked us to try to be loving and kind to everyone. When we fail, as we sometimes do, we need to put things right and be sincere; to be 'real' about what we are doing and saying. We should not act a part, as though we were wearing make-up.

It's not easy but it needs to be done. To be sincere and honest – really sorry – is the first step to putting things right. Then we can 'make up' (in another sense) with those we have hurt.

Table tale

Sam had never been in trouble at school before and as he sat outside the headteacher's door, waiting to be called inside, he put on a very brave face. When he got the message from the prefect to go to the head's room he told his mates that he didn't care. Now, as other pupils walked past and stared at him, he was very scared inside, but put on a bold, brave face for the passers-by. He hoped that they could not see he was trembling and really scared. He had prepared his story; he was going to say it was another boy's fault, definitely not his.

Then it happened; the door opened and he was invited in. The headteacher went and sat down behind his desk and Sam was left standing in front of the desk. The head reached into a drawer, took out a writing pad and picked up a pen and a pencil. 'Now,' he said, looking intently at Sam, 'you've never been in trouble before, have you, young man?'

'No,' muttered Sam.

'Well,' came the response, 'I can write your name on this pad in ink and keep it for ever as a record; or I could write your name in pencil, and if you remain good and well-behaved, I can rub it out in, say, six months' time. It is for you to choose. If you tell me honestly the whole truth, and assure me that you will not get into trouble again, it will be the pencil. If you start acting and telling me stories, it will be the pen and perhaps much worse. Which is it to be: pencil or pen?'

Sam came out of the room smiling. He had told the honest truth and said how sorry he was; he had promised that it would never happen again, and he meant it! Now he felt so much better. What his mum had always said was true (but he might not tell her): honesty is the best policy!

Table talk

It always seems easier to tell untruths and pretend, try to cover up what really happened. But usually we are found out, and then it's worse. Sam discovered that being open and honest is best, because you are not making things worse by adding lies to the problem, and people start to trust you. Trust is all-important. Can a person who tells lies ever really be trusted?

God talk

Dear God,
because you are open and generous and honest,
you want us to be the same.
You also want us to make up with people –
and with you –
when we have done wrong.
Please give us the courage and the strength
to do just that.

8
Make up (2)

Table time

Making up with friends and family, when we have done wrong, is fine, but it isn't the whole of it. When we hurt another person we hurt God. Jesus said very clearly, 'What you do to any one, you do to me.' So to be really nasty to a brother or sister is to be nasty to Jesus. And when we make up with another person, we also have to make up with God. There are two parts to being forgiven; God is only going to forgive us, and make up with us, if we forgive and make up with the other person.

Table tale

Mum had asked Sophie to wash up the dinner things, stacked on the draining board from the previous evening, while she put the washing out on the line in the garden. (The family had all gone straight out after the meal and were too tired to wash up when they had come home late.) When Mum came into the kitchen to prepare some breakfast, the washing-up was not touched. Sophie was in the lounge watching TV.

'Why haven't you done the washing up?' her mother asked from the lounge doorway.

'Not much point, is there?' called Sophie. 'All those plates will be dirty again soon.'

After a bit Sophie came into the kitchen looking for her breakfast. The table wasn't laid and her mother was putting away the crockery she had just dried.

'I'm hungry,' said Sophie. 'Where's my breakfast?'

'Not doing breakfast,' replied Mum. 'There's not much point, is there? You'll only be hungry again by lunchtime! There's your school bag. Off you go; you can get the early bus today.'

Table talk

Would Sophie's mum really have let her go to school without any breakfast? What point was she trying to make? By refusing to help her mother, Sophie hurt her, but she also hurt God at the same time because Jesus told us to love one another. Sophie failed to be loving and helpful. Just as plates have to be washed up every day after use, ready for a fresh start, so we too have to regularly say sorry to God and sorry to one another, and make a fresh start.

God talk

Kind and loving Father,
you want us to be kind and loving too.
When we fail and hurt you,
please help us to be quick to say sorry.
Amen.

9

Make up (3)

Table time

We sometimes hurt one another. Often we don't mean to do it but somehow it just happens. The wrong word slips out at the wrong moment, and even as it happens we realise we have done wrong. But it's impossible to un-say what has been said . . . and it's hard to say sorry. So often we turn away and make things worse. Adults as well as children can do that. If damage is done we need to make up and try to put right the harm done.

Table tale

Helen had two friends – boys – round to the house and they were all larking around in the lounge – lots of laughter and shrieks. Dad was in the kitchen helping to tidy up after tea. Suddenly there was a crash, and then silence. Dad ran to the lounge to see what had caused the shattering noise. The three children were sitting, hugging cushions and looking innocently at him, as he entered. On the floor, by the television set, was a smashed wall plate. It was one of a valuable set of four that Helen's dad had bought her mum for Christmas. When he saw the plate he was furious and shouted at the three children, 'Who broke the plate?'

There was no reply. So the question was directed at Helen: 'These are your friends. Who broke the plate?' The boys looked scared at the shouted questions and stared straight ahead.

Helen looked at her dad and said, in a soft voice, 'It just fell off the wall!' That did not improve things!

Her father said to the boys, 'Get your coats and get off home.' To Helen he said, 'Your room,' pointing to the stairs. 'We will talk more about this tomorrow, when I've cooled down.'

The next morning Helen entered the kitchen while her Dad was having his morning toast, and without another word said, 'I did it. We were throwing cushions around and mine hit the plate. I'm very sorry.' Her dad got up and put his arms around her and said, 'Thank you for owning up. I forgive you, but the plate cost £35 and you will have to pay from your savings for a new one to replace the one you broke.' When a replacement was found, Helen did pay for it.

Table talk

What do you think of that story? Notice there were two different things Helen's father said. He said, 'I forgive you', and then he told his daughter she had to put right the damage she had done. Is it right that Helen should have to pay to replace the plate?

Does God forgive us without expecting us to put things right?

God talk

Kind and generous Father,
your Son, Jesus, told us that you are always ready to forgive us,
but only if we are really and truly sorry.
And we are expected to forgive other people who may have hurt us.
Please help us to be ready to put right any harm we cause.
Amen.

10

Make up (4)

Table time

We often don't feel very sorry for doing wrong – committing sin –
because the things that we do are usually quite small and they can
seem unimportant. We think they're not worth worrying about.
This old traditional story suggests we are wrong about that.

Table tale

Two men went to visit a holy man for advice.

'Can you tell us what we must do to be forgiven our sins?'

'You must tell God that you are sorry,' said the holy man, 'and
he will forgive you.'

'We have done that,' replied one of the visitors, 'and still we
feel bad.'

'Tell me of your wrongdoing, my sons,' said the old man.

The first man said, 'I have committed a great and grievous sin.'

The second man said, 'I have done a lot of wrong things, but
they were all small and not important.'

'This is what you must do,' said the holy man. 'You must go
and get me a stone that represents each of your sins.'

The first man came back with a big stone and the second with a
bag of small stones.

'Now,' said the old man, 'take all those stones and put them
back where you found them.'

The first man picked up his big rock and staggered back to
where he had found it. But the second man could only remember
where a few of his pebbles had lain; he came back and said the
task was too difficult.

'You must know,' said the holy old man, 'that sins are like these

stones. If a person has committed a big sin, it lies like a heavy stone on his conscience; if he is truly sorry, he is forgiven and the load is taken away. But if a person is always doing small things that are wrong, he does not feel very guilty, so he is not sorry. So, you see, it is important to avoid little sins as well as big ones.
Anon

Table talk

When we make up with God, and with one another, we must remember the little things, like the unkind comment, or cutting remark; the sneaky dig in your brother/sister's back, the 50 pence taken from mum's purse without asking, or the insulting note passed in class while the teacher isn't watching. And so on. They may seem small but they add up and definitely need God's forgiveness.

God talk

Almighty God,
small can be beautiful,
but small can also be ugly.
Lots of small hurts to people
can make us unappealing and ugly to others.
Please help us to make up with you, and others,
for all the small things that we do regularly.
With your help we can improve.
Amen.

11
Wake up (1)

Table time

Some people walk in their sleep. When they wake up in the morning they have no memory of what they did. Other people sleepwalk through their lives, never clear about where they are going or the consequences of their actions. They find themselves in trouble of all kinds because they do not look ahead and foresee the outcome of what they do or want to do.

Table tale

Here is a traditional story from Italy.

A bright and clever young man, very pleased with his success at college, was telling his wise old grandfather about his plans for the future: 'I'm going to university to get a degree in Law.'

'And then?' his grandfather asked.

'I shall work hard and become a respected and famous lawyer,' replied the student.

'And then?' the old man enquired.

'Well, I will marry a beautiful woman and have a family, and live in a big imposing house.'

'And then?' asked the old gentleman.

'I will become rich and lots of celebrities will want me to be their lawyer.'

'And then?' the question came again.

'Then, well, then I suppose I will get older and eventually retire . . . but, of course, everyone who is anyone will know me.'

'And then?' the old man repeated.

The young man was getting irritated by the question. 'What do you mean by that?' he asked.

'I mean,' replied his grandfather, 'what happens next?'

'Well, I suppose I will die,' came the reply.

'And then?' persisted the old man. There was silence; the young man had no answer.

'Surely,' said the wise old man, 'now we come to the important part: how will your story end? Where will you be for all eternity? Will your life have won you a place in heaven or the other place?'

Table talk

Did the young man, do you think, wake up to what his grandfather was trying to get through to him? The 'And then?' question is a good one to remember. It can help us to wake up to the real situation we could be in. Say, for example, someone tells a lie to get out of trouble, then has to tell another lie, and another, to cover up. Then, as usually happens, they are found out! Trust has been destroyed; no one can be sure when the truth is being told and when it isn't. Asking ourselves, 'And then?' could be a wake-up call.

God talk

Loving Father,
all you want is for us to be happy.
May we find happiness by looking ahead
and seeing the consequences of our attitudes and actions.
We will then, Father, need your help to do the right thing.
Amen.

12
Wake up (2)

Table time

Sometimes an expected event wakes us up to a reality. One of the purposes of Lent is to have 40 days of 'purpose'; in other words, live deliberately for a time with serious thoughts about our present and our future.

Table tale

It was a shocking experience that made Alfred Nobel wake up. He opened a newspaper one morning to find an announcement of his death. Curious, he began to read it. The writer praised his success as a businessman and tried to estimate how much he was worth. The writer thought that Alfred would be best remembered as the man who developed dynamite! This shocked Alfred. His skills as a chemist had led to the development of a powder that could blow people up and kill them. He remembered how his own brother had died in an accidental explosion. He certainly did not want to be remembered, after his death, as the man who could cause death and destruction. Alfred made a plan and arranged for money to be available each year for five Nobel prizes. They are still awarded and perhaps the most famous is the Nobel Peace Prize. So Alfred's wish to be remembered for something good has come true.

Table talk

Everyone can be a power for good. Too often children and young people are given the impression by adults that their lives are about avoiding bad things. That's much too negative. There's so much more potential in each one of us; we are bundles of goodness that want 'unwrapping' or 'waking up'. Sometimes all that is needed is the wake-up call to the good we are capable of and the opportunity to prove it.

God talk

Father, we are all members of your family,
and all you want is for us to be happy,
and united to you, in love.
May we wake up to that call
and be the sort of children
that you want us to be.
Amen.

13
Get up (1)

Table time

Many times in the Gospel story Jesus says to sick people, 'Get up.'
'Get up, pick up your bed, and walk.'
'Little girl, I tell you to get up.'
Sometimes we have to say to ourselves, 'Come on, I've got to get up and make the effort.' As most of us are naturally lazy, it's always easier to sit around and do nothing than to get involved. But being a friend of Jesus is about doing things for others; it is about getting involved. To get up and get on with serving others is not easy, especially if we feel inadequate or burdened by our own worries and problems.

Table tale

A blind man and a lame man happened to come at the same time to a piece of very bad road. The former begged the latter to guide him through his difficulties. 'How can I do that,' said the lame man, 'as I am scarcely able to drag myself along? But if you were to carry me I can warn you about anything in the way; my eyes will be your eyes and your feet will be mine.' 'With all my heart,' replied the blind man. 'Let us serve one another.' So taking his lame companion on his back, they travelled in this way with safety and pleasure.
Aesop

Table talk

As Christians we are all called to 'serve one another in love' (Galatians 5:13), using our God-given talents and gifts. Should we be involved more in our local church and the local community? Have we had invitations to help in any way that we have declined or ignored?

God talk

In your family, Almighty Father,
there are always people in need of help and support:
the old, the sick, the lonely, the homeless.
We need to serve one another in love.
May we answer your call to get up and get involved,
for that is what your Son did,
and what he expects us, his friends, to do.
Amen.

14

Get up (2)

Table time

Life is like a journey. We are forever moving on. We cannot go back; we can only go forward. Sometimes it seems hard just to get up and go. We want to cling on to the past, or we worry too much about what the future may have in store for us instead of focusing on the present.

Table tale

There are two days in every week about which we should not worry, two days which should be kept free from fear and apprehension. One of these days is Yesterday with its mistakes and cares, its faults and blunders, its aches and pains. Yesterday has passed forever beyond our control. All the money in the world cannot bring back Yesterday. We cannot undo a single act we performed; we cannot erase a single word we said. Yesterday is gone. The other day we should not worry about is Tomorrow with its possible adversities, its burdens, its large promise and poor performance. Tomorrow is also beyond our immediate control. Tomorrow's sun will rise, either in splendour or behind a mask of clouds – but it will rise. Until it does, we have no stake in Tomorrow, for it is yet unborn. This leaves only one day – Today. Any man can fight the battles of just one day. It is only when you and I add the burdens of those two awful eternities – Yesterday and Tomorrow – that we break down. It is not the experience of Today that drives men mad – it is remorse or bitterness for something which happened Yesterday and the dread of what Tomorrow may bring.
Anon

Table talk

When we get up and set out on our journey of love we do not travel alone. We meet fellow Christians along the way, but more importantly we have a constant companion – Jesus, whose love stays the same yesterday, today and tomorrow. He promises to remain by our side whatever happens to us.

God talk

Life, Lord, is a journey,
and we have to get up and get on with it,
whatever happens.
Keep reminding us that we have your presence with us every step of the way.
May we place all our faith
in that loving presence and support.
Amen.

15
Pick up (1)

Table time

Just as we can do little things wrong – commit little sins – so we can do little things right! We are quite wrong to think that only big things matter. After Jesus had fed 5000 people he gave instructions that all the scraps should be picked up (Matthew 14:13-21). Our story today is about a man who picked up little things and by doing that he changed the lives of thousands of people.

Table tale

Elzéard Bouffier was a simple and uneducated shepherd, who lived in Provence, in France. In 1910, when his wife and son died, Elzéard went to live on his own in a very desolate and barren area, miles from anywhere. Tending his flock he had an idea. In the autumn he went looking for acorns and other nuts. He picked up and selected the strong healthy ones, which he stored. In the spring, while watching over his sheep, he planted out the nuts. He would prod a hole in the ground with his iron staff and drop in an acorn. He continued picking up and planting out, year after year, for 37 years. Gradually the whole barren land was transformed; the trees grew, undergrowth developed, all kinds of wildlife returned to the area and water became plentiful again. When Elzéard died in 1947 a whole region of Provence had totally changed; people moved into housing developments and enjoyed the protected parks and the beautifully wooded countryside.

Table talk

It is inspiring to learn what one man can do; how one person, with effort and determination, can pick up the smallest things of life and use them to change the lives of thousands. The very smallest things of our lives are important; for example, the smile you give someone can lift their spirits. What other small things can we 'pick up' and use, for God's glory, today?

God talk

Lord of Creation, Master and King,
nothing is small to you;
everything comes from your loving act of creation.
May we see your world as you see it,
and may we respect all that you have made.
May we use even the smallest things of our day
to bring you glory and praise.
Amen.

16
Pick up (2)

Table time

There is a long Christian tradition in believing that Jesus fell several times under the heavy weight of the cross as he carried it to Calvary. The Gospels tell us that Jesus was having such a hard time that a man from Cyrene, named Simon, was forced to pick up the cross and carry it for Jesus (Mark 15:21). Lots of people have burdens in life to carry, and perhaps we could help more if we noticed their need.

Table tale

This story appeared in the newspapers a little while ago.

Robert was born in Aldershot; his mother was Japanese and his father was a soldier in the British Army. When Robert started school, because he had black hair and looked Japanese, he was tormented by some of the other children, who called him names. When Christmas came round his parents gave him his first watch. Robert was very proud of his present and wore it to school, to show his teacher. At break time some older children took it from him and smashed it against a wall.

The school crossing lady asked Robert one day why he was walking to school, and crossing a very busy road, when he could use the school bus. Robert told her that his parents wanted him to use the bus but he was frightened of the other children because they pulled his hair and called him rude names. Robert walked to school for nearly a whole term, until one day, while crossing the road, he was knocked down by a car and killed.

Table talk

Who killed Robert? The car driver? Or was it someone else, perhaps a group of people? It is so sad when you hear of school children who die because they are bullied at school. Do we know anyone who is bullied? If we do, shouldn't we be like Simon and pick up their 'load'; be there for them and support them. Simon must have been unpopular with the crowd that stood in the streets jeering at Jesus, but whom do we still talk about today, Simon or individual members of the crowd?

God talk

Merciful Father,
you must have been so sad
at what people did to your Son, Jesus.
Tragically, people still treat innocent and harmless individuals cruelly.
May we be like Simon,
ready and prepared to pick up the burdens carried by others;
to be there for anyone in need.
Amen.

17

Grow up (1)

Table time

We never stop growing up. Grown-ups have to carry on growing up, although not in the same way as children do. There are different parts to a human being. There's the body part and that carries on developing and growing until a person is about 20. But there are other parts to a human being – for example, feelings and thoughts. Some people who are grown-up in their bodies are not grown-up in their feelings, thoughts or their values. A grown-up can act very childishly.

One good thing about belonging to a family is that in the family we can, in a safe place, show and express our feelings. In a family, too, we can learn how to be loving and kind and all the other values necessary for a happy life. Here's a story, written a long time ago, long before *Toy Story*. Like *Toy Story* it is set in a child's bedroom or nursery.

Table tale

The Skin Horse had lived longer in the nursery than any of the others. He was so old that his brown coat was bald in patches and showed the seams underneath, and most of the hairs in his tail had been pulled out to string bead necklaces. He was wise, for he had seen a long succession of mechanical toys arrive to boast and swagger, and by-and-by break their mainsprings and pass away, and he knew that they were only toys, and would never turn into anything else. For nursery magic is very strange and wonderful, and only those playthings that are old and wise and experienced like the Skin Horse understand all about it.

'What is REAL?' asked the Rabbit one day, when they were

lying side by side near the nursery fender, before Nana came to tidy the room. 'Does it mean having things that buzz inside you and a stick-out handle?'

'Real isn't how you are made,' said the Skin Horse. 'It's a thing that happens to you. When a child loves you for a long, long time, not just to play with, but REALLY loves you, then you become Real.'

'Does it hurt?' asked the Rabbit.

'Sometimes,' said the Skin Horse, for he was always truthful. 'When you are Real you don't mind being hurt.'

'Does it happen all at once, like being wound up,' he asked, 'or bit by bit?'

'It doesn't happen all at once,' said the Skin Horse. 'You become. It takes a long time. That's why it doesn't happen often to people who break easily, or have sharp edges, or who have to be carefully kept. Generally, by the time you are Real, most of your hair has been loved off, and your eyes drop out and you get loose in the joints and very shabby. But these things don't matter at all, because once you are Real you can't be ugly, except to people who don't understand.'

from *The Velveteen Rabbit* by Margery Williams

Table talk

Do we have any teddies or toys in our home that we have loved so much that they have become 'real'? If we think about people, rather than toys, what is someone like who 'breaks easily' or 'has sharp edges'?

God wants us to be REAL. That means he wants us to put all our energy into being loving and not too much energy into worrying about what we look like or what people think of us. Lent is a time that helps us to do that.

God talk

Loving Father,
you want us to be real people;
people who put loving first
and not people who break easily or have sharp edges.
Help us to use our giving up and our taking up this Lent
to become more real every day.
Amen.

18
Grow up (2)

Table time

Lots of young people have secret fears inside them. They carry around worries about how they look, compared with other people. They are not mature enough to accept themselves as they are, rejoicing in their difference from others.

Table tale

Once upon a time there were three bugs, Billy, Bobby and Brian. All three were going to the same party. Each of them was worried. Billy had noticed earlier that day that his right antenna was a little shorter than his left. He was sure that the other bugs would notice and tease him. Bobby was dreading the party; his antennae were curled a little at the ends. They weren't, he thought, as straight as other bugs' antennae. Brian was worried because he felt that his antennae stuck out at an odd angle to his head.

All three bugs dreaded the thought of being embarrassed. All the other bugs were having a great time at the party, but three of them weren't. Billy kept himself apart in a corner. He spent most of his time trying to hide his antennae; he wished they were more like Bobby's or Brian's. Meanwhile Bobby kept looking around, hoping desperately that no one would notice his antennae and wishing his were more like Billy's or Brian's. Brian, too, was feeling very self-conscious and hating every minute of the party. If only he could be as good-looking as Billy and Bobby. All three really wanted to have a good time and make new friends but instead went home miserable because they could not stop worrying.

Table talk

Some people are so self-conscious and concerned about unreal fears that they ruin their lives. Being 'grown-up' is about accepting ourselves as we are and realising that other people are more interested in what we are like inside, our personality and character, than the shape of our nose or the size of our ears. We are as God has made us and intended us to be; we should rejoice in our uniqueness.

God talk

Creator Father,
you have made us to be unique individuals.
Help us to appreciate the life you have given us.
Help us to accept ourselves as we are,
with our looks, our capabilities and our gifts.
May we always appreciate all your gifts to us.
Amen.

19
Grow up (3)

Table time

It is so easy to be selfish, to grab the best for yourself. That is how we start as little babies, believing that the whole world revolves around us. It isn't surprising because a new baby in a family is made the centre of attention and everyone fusses around. Gradually, as time passes and we grow, we realise that there are other people about who are equally as important as us. We have to grow up from being totally self-centred to a point where we can generously and cheerfully share with others, and give up the best place to someone else.

Table tale

Two year-old Sharon and her friend Michael, who was nearly 4, were playing happily in the garden. Suddenly their mums, who were enjoying a quiet cup of coffee in the kitchen, were disturbed by a great commotion. Rushing to the window they saw both children trying to jam themselves, at the same time, on the seat of the one and only tricycle. After much shouting and screeching both managed to squeeze on, but neither could move and nor could the tricycle! When their mums got to them Sharon was sobbing and Michael was stoutly and loudly proclaiming, 'If one of us gets off *I* could ride it properly.' It was resolved that they would take turns. Michael had the first short ride up the concrete garden path, pursued after less than 30 seconds by Sharon, calling, 'Me turn, me turn.'

Table talk

Neither the 2-year-old nor even the 4-year-old in that story had learnt how to share. If helped by good example in the home, it develops gradually. How good are we, in our home, at sharing? Are any of us quite bodily 'grown-up' but still at the baby-end of being able to share and share generously not grudgingly. Perhaps our giving up/taking up this Lent will help us.

God talk

You have shown us, Lord Jesus,
that true happiness comes from sharing generously,
not from being self-centred and selfish.
Please help us because it is so natural for us
to think only of ourselves;
with your help we can be more generous.
Amen.

20
Clean up (1)

Table time

Many years ago, in the age of our grandparents, there was no gas or electric central heating with radiators in bedrooms, bathrooms and so on. There were coal fires, which caused a lot of smoke. When the dark, cold days of winter were finished and spring arrived with lighter, brighter days, people would spring-clean their homes. It was an opportunity for a fresh start, and they took it. Remember that the word 'Lent' comes from the old English for spring. Lent is a time for spring-cleaning.

Table tale

The Mole had been working very hard all morning, spring-cleaning his little home. First with brooms, then with dusters; then on ladders and steps and chairs, with a brush and a pail of whitewash; till he had dust in his throat and eyes, and splashes of whitewash all over his black fur, and an aching back and weary arms. Spring was moving in the air above and in the earth below and around him, penetrating even his dark and lowly little house with its spirit of divine discontent and longing. It was small wonder, then, that he suddenly flung down his brush on the floor, said 'Bother!' and 'O blow!' and also 'Hang spring-cleaning!' and bolted out of the house without even waiting to put on his coat. Something up above was calling him imperiously . . . So he scraped and scratched and scrabbled and scrooged and then he scrooged again and scrabbled and scratched and scraped, working busily with his little paws and muttering to himself, 'Up we go! Up we go!' till at last, pop! his snout came out into the sunlight and he found himself rolling in the warm grass of a great meadow.

from *The Wind in the Willows* by Kenneth Grahame

Table talk

Mole said, 'Up we go! Up we go!' That's surely why we do a little spring-cleaning in our lives during Lent, so that we too can go up and be more firmly in God's presence and favour. How do we clean up or spring-clean?

God talk

Loving God,
you want us to be like you and imitate you;
you want us to be loving and kind.
But we so often fail to love.
Help us to clean up our lives,
so that we can rise up above our selfishness
and give you and our neighbour
the love which is their due.
Amen.

21
Clean up (2)

Table time

Are we sincere? Jesus had a go at people who were hypocrites, people who said one thing but did something different. He told the short and dramatic parable of the man who criticised his brother for having a speck of sawdust in his eye, while he had a plank in his own eye! (Matthew 7:3)

Table tale

The class of Year 9 pupils were roused to indignation; they were shooting their hands up and getting told off for calling out comments. They had been hearing about slavery in the nineteenth century; about how David Livingstone and other Christians had struggled to get freedom and dignity for the slaves; how men, women and children had been forced to work for other people.

'You mean they had to clean up after the rich people, do things for them and wait on them. It's disgusting, really bad,' said one girl.

At that moment the deputy head came into the classroom. 'I have an important notice for you all. If there is still loads of litter lying about on the tennis courts after lunch today, there will be an after-school detention for whole classes.'

'That's ridiculous,' a boy called out, 'a detention for dropping litter! The school should pay a man to pick the litter up.' The deputy head spent a few more minutes speaking to the class and then she left.

The RE teacher asked, 'Have you ever heard of the word "hypocrite"?' When there was no response he said, 'A lot of you are hypocrites, because one minute you are condemning slavery and saying how bad it is that the slaves had to wait on the rich, and the next minute you are refusing to pick up your litter and wanting to get a man to wait on you by picking it up. It's not just the tennis courts that want cleaning up, it's your set of values.'

Table talk

Why should anyone have to clean up our mess? It is very unfair to expect anyone to act as our servant or slave. In a family lots of jobs have to be done; if one person is doing the clothes wash, then another must do their share by helping to clean the house or put dishes away, or help with the shopping. No one, but no one, has the right to sit around and do nothing, or very little.

God talk

At the Last Supper, Lord Jesus,
you got up from the table
and washed the feet of your friends.
You said, 'What I have done for you,
you should do for one another.'
You gave us an example of humble service.
May each of us round this table
take our turn in serving one another,
never leaving one person to clean up after us.
Amen.

22

Stand up (1)

Table time

Around the world last year over 930 people died because they were Christians, friends of Jesus! They stood up for their Christian faith and were killed because they had the courage to be Christians. It is easy to be a secret Christian, not letting on to anyone what you believe, but sometimes it takes real guts to admit what you believe and be proud of your beliefs.

Table tale

A few years ago, on a bright spring day in April, three senior students, dressed all in black, entered their school, Columbine High School, and started shooting their fellow students. In their hate-filled rage they targeted black students, athletes and Christians. They killed 12 students and one teacher, and wounded 23 others, before shooting themselves.

Cassie Bernall, a beautiful 17-year-old, had gone to the library to do some study. When the shooting started she hid under a table. Eric Harris, one of the gun-carrying students, slapped the table under which Cassie was hiding and told her to come out. When she did, he pointed his gun at her head and asked, 'Do you believe in God?' Cassie said, 'Yes.' Eric laughed, pulled the trigger and killed her.

After the shooting Cassie's parents found a book she had been reading. She had underlined a sentence: 'All of us should live life so as to be able to face eternity at any time.'

Table talk

Cassie was a modern martyr; she was only 17 but she was prepared to die for her faith. What we are trying to do for Lent is pretty small change compared to her courage and sacrifice. Could we say 'yes' to being a Christian, if we were threatened?

God talk

Almighty God,
for her belief in you, Cassie died.
We are not likely to be asked to die for you,
but please help us to live for you, generously and bravely.
Amen.

23
Stand up (2)

Table time

One of the hardest things for a young person is to admit to their mates – their peer group – that they are a Christian and their faith means a lot to them. And yet that is what Christ, our friend, asks us to do. We are not a secret organisation but a community with a wonderful message of love and hope for our society. The last request of Jesus, before he left this earth, was that we would all have the courage to tell others about his Good News. 'Go out,' he said, 'into the whole world and share the Good News.' And he promised to be with his friends who tried to do that.

Table tale

A student was asked to do a piece of homework on 'A Missionary'. This is what she wrote.

When I was asked to write about a missionary a few people crossed my mind, like Mother Teresa, then I stopped and thought, I can't write about one of these great people because I don't really know them. It's true I've heard their names and read a bit about them, but I don't know what they're like. The person I think is a missionary, and a good one, is my mother. This may sound peculiar but surely you don't have to be a nun or a priest to be a missionary. My mum's mission is to be a housewife and a mother to me and my family. My mum has never been selfish and put herself before her family. I have never wanted for anything and I've never been without her endless love. Like the famous missionaries, my mother has needed a lot of courage at times, but she has always been there for me and my brothers. She is really respected in our neighbourhood because she helps with all sorts of charity fund-raising events. And her church is very important to her, too. I am very lucky to have a missionary mother.

Table talk

Would you agree that that girl's mother is a real missionary? How can she be a missionary if she isn't out preaching and telling people about Christ and his message, or is she doing it a different way? How could we be better missionaries?

God talk

Almighty God,
your Son taught us to call you 'Father'.
May we, as your children, be prepared to show your love
to neighbours and friends.
May we, by the power of good example,
spread the message of your love.
Amen.

24
Stand up (3)

Table time

It is important to stand up for your beliefs, but sometimes we have to stand up for others. There are many people in our world who have no voice – well, they have a voice, of course, but they can't use it to stand up for themselves. Examples would be the millions in the world who live in countries where they are forbidden by their government to speak up; or the many millions of people in terrible poverty; or the many children and young people who are sold into slavery every week of the year. Here's the story of one, who could not stand up for herself.

Table tale

Binlah is now free and happy but when she was 11 years old she became a slave. Binlah lived with her family in a village called Korat in north-east Thailand. The family was very poor, so when a smartly dressed businessman from Bangkok arrived by car they were very interested to hear of the work he could get for Binlah in the big city. Assured that she would be well cared for and have a good job in a restaurant, Binlah's father accepted £85 as an advance on her wages. (He realised later that that was the price he had sold her for.)

In Bangkok, 300 miles from home, Binlah was re-sold by the agent at a profit to the owner of an ice cream factory. She was shown the machine that she had to work and the dirty mattress alongside it where she was to sleep. Binlah had to start work at five in the morning and did not finish each day until midnight. She received one meal a day and had to eat and sleep where she worked.

Later she told how the man would hit her to make her work faster, and how she cried herself to sleep each night. Fortunately for Binlah her mattress was beside the corrugated sheeting which formed the wall of the factory and her crying, each night, could be heard by a poor family who lived close by the factory. They were disturbed, and found and spoke to a representative of the Save the Children Agency. The charity arranged to buy back the brutally beaten and half-starved 11-year-old. After a period in hospital Binlah was reunited with her family.

Table talk

Binlah was very lucky. People spoke up for her. If they hadn't she would have been dead within the year. Now, as we talk about it, there are hundreds of thousands of children in slavery and work conditions like that. Can we make it part of our Lent that we look for an opportunity to stand up for those who cannot stand up for themselves?

God talk

Lord,
we are horrified to know that so many of your children,
whom you love and care about,
are used and abused by people to make money.
May we do all we can to stand up for these little ones.
Help us to find ways of standing up for those in slavery.
Amen.

25
Cheer up (1)

Table time

There are no stories in the Gospels of Jesus being miserable; angry in the Temple, yes; terrified in the Garden of Gethsemane, yes; sad because a friend had died, yes. Miserable, never. In fact he told his friends to be cheerful when they gave things up or took on new activities. Jesus said, 'When you give up food, don't look miserable but look bright and fresh, so that no one will know you are giving up anything' (Matthew 6:16).

Table tale

'There was a little Asian girl at school today. And she's going to be my friend,' a 6-year-old boy told his dad. 'Does she speak English?' his father enquired. 'No,' came the reply, 'but it doesn't matter because she laughs in English.'
Anon

Table talk

Not long ago a newspaper reported that a 6-year-old laughs about 300 times a day, but most grown-ups do it only 47 times. And there are some sad individuals who only manage six times a day! Do we laugh enough? And have enough fun together?

God talk

God of joy and laughter,
you made us to be happy.
Help us to do things for you in Lent with a smile,
and do all we can to cheer up people who are sad.
Amen.

26
Cheer up (2)

Table time

One of the signs of being a Christian is living with a sense of joy, and trying to help others to have that same joy in their lives. There's another target for us for Lent!

Table tale

Two 10-year-old boys found themselves in hospital. They were strangers to one another and shared the same room off the main ward. Simon, placed by the only window, was the fitter of the two, although, like Martin, he could only leave his bed with the assistance of a nurse. At first Martin, in the bed by the door, was very poorly, unhappy and quite depressed. Simon worked hard at trying to cheer him up, and he succeeded. As he gained in strength Martin was entertained, all day, every day, by his new friend, who brightened up each day with vivid descriptions of what he could see from the window alongside his bed. Simon told Martin of the daffodils coming out in the park across the street, told him about the children playing on the swings and round-about, told him about the old and young people passing in the street below.

The sad day came when the boys were parted. Simon was sent off for convalescence and they promised to stay in touch. As soon as Simon had gone Martin asked to be moved to the bed by the window. The staff nurse, mysteriously, would not permit it! She gave good reasons but, as the bed stayed empty, Martin asked again and again. A few days later a new nurse was on duty and Martin asked again. He was moved. With eager anticipation Martin looked out of the window. He looked and looked again in stunned disbelief. There was nothing there but a blank brick wall and at its foot a squalid yard with a row of dustbins. Then Martin appreciated the love of his friend. For over a month Simon had worked hard to cheer Martin up with his vivid imagination. And he had succeeded.

Table talk

That's what Lent and Easter is about: putting ourselves out for others. Jesus did it in an extreme way, even to death. We have to do it, too, to improve people's lives.

God talk

Father,
your Son put himself out for us
in the most generous way possible.
May we seek, even in the smallest ways,
to put ourselves out for others.
May we try to brighten lives
by being positive and cheerful.
Amen.

27
Cheer up (3)

Table time

Do we take life too seriously? When you spend time looking, really looking, at individuals in a crowd of people, you wonder if God wasn't having a laugh when he created human beings! Where was Jesus when he worked his first miracle? In the Temple praying, in the synagogue preaching, or discussing religious ideas with a group of serious rabbis? No, he was having a good time at a party! The supply of wine had run out and Jesus fixed it! (Water into wine.) Where was his last miracle worked? Yes, at a party; his Passover meal – which included dancing and singing – with his Apostles. (Wine into blood.)

Table tale

Paddy died and went to stand in the queue for heaven. He was well back in the line and kept seeing people turned away, to make their journey to another place. As he got closer to the front of the queue he could see St Peter checking each person against entries in his book. Paddy thought, 'I've got no really good actions recorded; I've not been visiting the sick or feeding the hungry; I can't think of anything I've done for others. It's the other place for me!'

At last, with great dread, Paddy stood at the front of the queue. St Peter looked long and hard at his book and then broke into a smile. 'Come into heaven, Paddy, because in life you used your great gift of humour to make people laugh at your terrible jokes. That brightened up and saved more people than you will ever know. Welcome to heaven.'

Table talk

Some people can remember jokes and some can't. Some people have the gift of laughter and the ability to cheer others up. Whether we have the special gift or not, we can all make an effort to cheer one another up when the need arises. Joy is the sign of the Christian.

God talk

Heavenly Father,
one of the gifts of the Holy Spirit is joy.
Please give us this gift.
We do not ask for ourselves,
but so that we can light up other people's lives
and bring them your peace and joy.
Amen.

28
Reach up (1)

Table time

We live in a world that pushes the idea that you can only get on and be successful – even a celebrity – if you are assertive, pushy and up there with the cool bunch. That is not the teaching we get from Jesus. He is the greatest celebrity of all time (we even date our time from his birth), but he was never bossy, pushy or assertive. He said, 'Learn of me, because I am gentle and humble.' Not an easy target to reach up to.

Table tale

The wind and the sun, so the fable goes, once had a quarrel. The wind boasted that he was much stronger, more powerful and more important than the sun. He said, 'You are much too meek and gentle. I'll show you what power I have, and how much stronger I am than you. See that old man over there, with a big coat on? You see how I get him to take it off; I can do it much quicker than you can.'

'All right,' said the sun, 'we'll see.' So the sun went behind a cloud, but left a little hole so that he could peep through and see what the wind did. The wind blew and blew as hard as he could, causing a terrible storm, but the harder he blew, the tighter the man wrapped his coat around him. In the end the poor old wind had to become calm and give in.

Then it was the sun's turn. He came out from behind the cloud and smiled gently on the old man. After a little while the old man began to wipe his forehead with his handkerchief; then he pulled his coat off.

So gentleness beat powerful force.

Table talk

Is it better to learn from a TV celebrity, who may be completely forgotten in a few years' time, or from Jesus? His way is more difficult. We have to reach up to the targets he sets – like loving people who we don't get on with, or being gentle, humble and kind. Surely if we don't reach up to higher standards and values, we will sink back.

God talk

Father, your Son set us high standards;
he expected us to reach up to higher values.
It is hard for us, Lord,
because not everyone sees that being gentle and humble
is more important than being forceful and assertive.
Help us to live by the way of our Saviour.
Amen

29
Reach up (2)

Table time

The big thing in schools, offices and other places of work is having targets – something for pupils, students and adults at work to aim for. What do we aim for, as friends and disciples of Jesus? In Lent perhaps we should examine our Christian targets.

Table tale

A little girl was taken by her parents to visit one of the old cathedrals in our country. The family joined a guided tour of the cathedral. As the guide was explaining a historic tomb nearby, the girl was staring at a great stained-glass window, through which the summer sun was streaming, bathing the cathedral floor in colour. As the group was about to move on she asked the guide in a shrill, clear voice, 'Who are those people in the pretty window?'

'Those are the saints,' the man replied.

That night as she was undressing for bed she told her mother, 'I know who the saints are.'

'Do you, dear?' replied her mother. 'Who are they?'

'They are the people who let the light shine through.'

Table talk

Surely our target should be to aim to be what Jesus wants us to be. He wants us to be loving people; people who love God with our whole heart and our whole self. And people who love our neighbours as we love ourselves. Then, if we hit the target, we will be people through whom the light of God will pour. It may be embarrassing to say it but our target is to be saints.

God talk

You have lofty plans for us, dear God.
You want us to try hard to be loving people,
loving you and loving others.
In other words you want us to try to be saints.
It's a lofty plan, Lord, but a target to keep in mind.
Amen.

30
Fed up (1)

Table time

We all get a little fed up sometimes. It is impossible, as human beings, to be bouncy and positive all the time, although we ought to try. We get tired sometimes and then, perhaps, we get a bit grumpy. The people who we live with are prepared to make allowances, as long as we don't take it out on others.

Table tale

Do you know the song *Nellie the Elephant?** The words are these:

Nellie the elephant packed her trunk
and said goodbye to the circus.
Off she went with a trumpety trump,
trump, trump, trump.

Nellie got fed up with the way she was treated in the circus and decided to run away.

*Ralph Butler/Peter Hart © Copyright 1956 Dash Music Company Ltd.

Table talk

That is just a children's song, but sadly there are teenagers who, when they get fed up, run away, always to deeper and more serious problems. Running away, turning our back on someone or something, is not the way.

Jesus got very fed up in the Garden of Gethsemane. His Father wanted him to make a sacrifice of himself, and all Jesus could see ahead was intense pain and utter rejection. It would have been easy for Jesus to slip away in the darkness of the Garden; no one would have missed him for hours. He could have returned to his old job and life in Nazareth. No, even while he sweated blood, he refused to run away; Jesus stopped and faced the pain and rejection. If he had slipped off in the dark there would be no Lent, no Easter and no Christian Church.

God talk

Father, because we are human,
we sometimes get fed up.
Please give us a helping hand at those times,
so that we don't take it out on others
and make them unhappy.
May we always imitate Jesus,
who did not run away from his problems,
but faced them
and brought upon himself the glory due to him.
Amen.

31
Fed up (2)

Table time

Everyone wants to be happy. That's one thing every human being has in common. But people look for happiness in all sorts of ways. One misguided way, in our society, is to believe you find happiness by having more and more things, the latest and best of every new product. That is not the Christian understanding. Happiness is found not in what you have but in who you are.

Table tale

Here is an ancient tale about looking for happiness.

Once upon a time there was a medieval king who asked for advice from a wise old man at his court. The king was very fed up and depressed; he just could not cheer himself up. He kept thinking about all his worries and troubles. So he called for the wise man and asked him how he might find happiness. 'I want to be really happy,' the king said.

The old man replied, 'There is only one cure for the king. His Majesty must sleep one night in the shirt of a happy man.'

Messengers were dispatched by the king to search for a man who was truly happy. But everyone who was approached had some anxiety and worry to spoil their happiness. At long last they found a beggar, who sat smiling by the roadside; he said that he was a really happy man with no worries. The messengers offered him a very large sum of money for his shirt. The beggar burst into uncontrollable laughter, and replied. 'I am sorry, I cannot help the king. I haven't got a shirt to sell him.'

Table talk

The beggar had nothing and was perfectly happy; the king had everything, except happiness. Having things doesn't necessarily bring happiness; in fact, having lots of things can cause real unhappiness. How is this true?

God talk

God of all hopefulness,
God of all joy,
may we not look for happiness
from having possessions and the latest of things,
but seek true happiness from loving you,
and caring for others.
Amen.

32
Raise up (1)

Table time

Years ago there used to be a collection of wise descriptions of what Christians believe and do. In it there was this description of prayer: 'Prayer is the raising up of the mind and heart to God.' Many people believe that to be an excellent description of prayer. We can't journey through Lent without some thoughts on prayer.

Table tale

One day a boy of 5 was left alone with his father at bedtime. It had never happened before because Dad usually got home from work after the little boy was in bed. After his bath and some fun together the boy got his pyjamas on. His father was just about to lift him into bed when the little boy said, 'Daddy, I have to say my prayers first.' He knelt down by his bed and prayed, 'Now I lay me down to sleep, I pray the Lord my soul to keep . . .' When he had finished his usual prayers he looked at his dad, and carried on praying, 'Dear God, make me a great big good man, like my daddy. Amen.'

In a moment he was in bed, and in five minutes he was asleep. And then his father knelt by his son's bed and prayed, 'Dear Lord, make me a great big good man, like my boy thinks I am.'

Table talk

Jesus prayed and he taught his friends to pray. He suggested that prayer should be done in private. Do we pray in private or only when we do it together? How can we use Lent to improve our prayer? Any ideas?

God talk

Heavenly Father, you want us to talk to you,
to build our friendship with you
through sharing not just our wants and our needs
but our joys and excitements,
our plans and our hopes for the future.
May we make a renewed effort to give time and energy
to raising our minds and hearts to you.
Amen.

33
Raise up (2)

Table time

When the weather is beautiful and we are out in the countryside, it is easy to see what a beautiful planet we live on. It isn't so easy on a bleak miserably wet day! However, whatever the weather we all know that there is much beauty on this earth. Our prayer should recognise and acknowledge that. Our Creator God deserves our thanks and our praise. We need once in a while – and Lent is a perfect time – to raise up our thoughts above the little irritating worries and anxieties of each day and try to see the bigger picture.

Table tale

On either side of Rat and Mole, as they glided onwards, the rich meadow-grass seemed that morning of a freshness and a greenness unsurpassable. Never had they noticed the roses so vivid, the willow-herb so riotous, the meadow-sweet so odorous and pervading. Then the murmur of the approaching weir began to hold the air, and they felt a consciousness that they were nearing the end, whatever it might be, that surely awaited their expedition.

Slowly, but with no doubt or hesitation whatever, and in something of a solemn expectancy, the two animals passed through the broken tumultuous water and moored their boat at the flowery margin of the island. In silence they landed, and pushed through the blossom and scented herbage and undergrowth . . .'This is the place of my song-dream, the place the music played to me,' whispered the Rat, as if in a trance. 'Here, in this holy place, here if anywhere, surely we shall find Him.'

Then suddenly the Mole felt a great Awe fall upon him, an awe that turned his muscles to water, bowed his head, and rooted his feet to the ground.

from *The Wind in the Willows* by Kenneth Grahame

Table talk

That's only part of a lovely passage in *The Wind in the Willows;* it all merits reading, because, although not particularly Christian, it can help to awaken in us the awe that Rat and Mole experienced. If we realise the beauty of God's creation and all he has done for us, then we will want to raise up our thoughts and our prayers of thanks and praise to him.

God talk

Awe-inspiring Creator God,
to look at the night sky
or the scenic beauties of nature
prompts us to say,
'Whoa, how incredibly great and wonderful you are.'
We raise up our hearts and minds to say,
all glory and praise and honour be to you,
now and always.
Amen.

34
Offer up (1)

Table time

We can never know how things in the future are going to develop, what will happen and how it will happen. Very often what we do today affects what happens tomorrow or the day after or some time in the future.

Table tale

There is a legend about the boy who offered up his five barley loaves and two small fish so that Christ could feed the great crowd. It tells how the boy hurried home, after all the fragments had been collected up, and told his mother about the exciting incident. With eyes still big with the wonder of it, he told her how his five little barley loaves and the two dried fish had multiplied in the Saviour's hand until there was enough to satisfy 5000 hungry people. And then, with a wistful look, he added, 'I wonder, Mum, whether it would be like that with everything you gave him.'

Table talk

There is an old Christian custom of saying Morning Prayers, not one that all Christians still practise. This is a great pity because it is a very good practice to offer the day to God, right at its beginning, before we have any idea how it will turn out. The boy in our story makes the point that the good we do, if offered to God, our loving Father, as a prayer, will multiply and have unforeseen effects, for ourselves and those we love.

God talk

Little things are of value to you, O God;
let us not forget it.
I offer to you
all the little things I do or say or think today
as little prayers of love and praise.
Amen.

35
Offer up (2)

Table time

As we approach the end of Lent we need to think a little about 'sacrifice' –'offering up' a gift. On Good Friday we remember the sacrifice that Jesus made; he offered up himself to God, his almighty Father.

Table tale

There is a story told about hospitality – that is, giving the best welcome you can to visitors. It comes from the Bedouin of the Sahara desert. The Sahara is a vast, desolate place, hundreds of miles of barren wilderness, some, but not all of which is sand. It is the home of the Touareg and other Bedouin tribes.

One band of eight Touareg, with their camels, had been days out in the desert and their food supply had run out. After three more days they were very hungry and desperate to find something to eat. Then in the early morning light one of the Bedouin caught sight, at a distance, of a desert hare. Immediately the group mounted up and set out in pursuit of the animal. Towards evening, with great delight, they caught it. They made camp and started to prepare the much-awaited food. The stew was almost ready when on the horizon appeared a group of riders, six men who were not Touareg but from another rather hostile tribal group. The hearts and stomachs of those around the fire dropped into their boots; they knew what they were expected to do, and hospitality, even to enemies, demanded it. When the visitors rode up to the fire, the Touareg stood, bowed and invited the travellers to 'come and partake of our humble meal'. They did, while the hungry hunters of the hare stood back from the fire and watched.

When the meal was finished the six visitors stood, bowed to the hosts, thanked them profusely and said their goodbyes. The Touareg went to bed hungry.

Table talk

The hospitality of the desert obliged the Touareg to put their own needs last and offer up their much-needed food to travellers, who were certainly not friends. The sacrifice was made, and it cost them, and it was accepted. Jesus offered up to his Father the best gift that he had: his own life. He gave it up freely, but very painfully, for us. That's true love.

God talk

Merciful and loving Father,
your Son Jesus the Christ
offered himself up to you.
We know you accepted his gift
because he rose from the dead.
May we be generous in making sacrifices
and look for ways of helping others.
Amen.

36
Offer up (3)

Table time

We are making rather a lot of 'offering up' in our preparation for Easter because that is the very centre of the message of the death and resurrection of Jesus. He offered up himself as a gift to his Father, and his gift was received and celebrated by the resurrection. Lots of ordinary people make sacrifices every day for those they love, and their example can be an inspiration to us.

Table tale

St Mark's High School was organising a pilgrimage to the Holy Land, and the RE teacher called a meeting for all those who wanted to go. There was a good response and letters were given out to be taken home to parents, giving the dates, the cost and all the other details. Sophie hung around at the end of the meeting to speak privately to the teacher. 'It's a lot of money,' she commented. 'I desperately want to go but I don't know how we can afford it.'

The teacher knew Sophie's mum was on her own, trying to bring up three children, and made a suggestion. 'Why don't you leave it for now and go in a few years' time when you are at work and can save up for it?' Sophie was clearly not impressed by that suggestion, but thanked the teacher and left.

The next day Sophie sought out the teacher and said, 'My mum saw how much I wanted go to the Holy Land and said I could go.'

Her teacher asked, 'How will she manage to do that?'

Sophie said, 'I've promised to baby-sit my brother and sister while Mum takes on an evening job at the local pub for five nights a week.'

Table talk

Isn't that love in action? Sophie's mum could see how important it was to her and what a good thing it was, so she offered to give up her evenings for nine months, while they raised the money. A real sacrifice was being made by Sophie's mum, just as Jesus made a very much bigger one for each of us.

God talk

Heavenly Father,
you asked your Son to offer himself up;
he did it for love of you.
You ask us to show our love for others
by making sacrifices to help and support them;
please help us with this
because we don't find it at all easy.
Amen.

37
Eat up (1)

Table time

In the prayer Jesus taught us we say, 'Give us this day our daily bread.' We don't really notice the words because we always have enough food, so we don't even think about the need to pray for it. But not everyone in the world is so fortunate.

Table tale

A missionary priest, just returned from Africa, told the story of how he looked out of his window one day and saw a young African boy swinging to and fro on a old swing made with a rope and half a car tyre. The swing was across the road from the priest's garden. All afternoon the boy played there on his own, until the priest, feeling he ought to be getting home, walked across the road to speak to the 10-year-old. As the priest left his garden he snapped a large mango off the tree standing there. When he crossed the road he tossed the mango to the boy and stood to chat to him. After a few minutes he said, 'Aren't you going to eat the mango?' The boy said, 'No, I'll take it home now. It's not my turn to eat today.'

Table talk

'It's not my turn to eat today.' There's a boy who knew what hunger was; he could really pray, 'Give us today something to eat.' Think of the wide range of food we have, here, in this house. Think how fussy and picky some people can be, about different flavours of crisps, for example. One of the aims of Lent is to alert us to the very serious needs of others and to give in charity to them. In our *God talk* let's say the Lord's Prayer very slowly and with meaning.

God talk

Our Father, who art in heaven . . .

38
Eat up (2)

Table time

The last thing that Jesus did with his friends was share a meal. That's what we humans do when we want to celebrate; we go out for a meal, have a big family meal or a party. When we go to church and share in the Eucharist, which is a meal but much more than a meal, we share with others. We cannot share the bread and wine of the Eucharist without being aware of how important it is to have enough to eat.

Table tale

The parish of Shoeburyness in Essex is twinned with a parish in South Africa. The priest in South Africa, Father Hector, has a vast parish, almost the size of Essex, to look after, and some of his people are very poor.

Just before last Christmas, the English parish sent £200 to Father Hector and asked him to give some of his poor children a treat for Christmas. Two weeks after Christmas this letter arrived.

'I am sending you two photos of the excited children that you gave Christmas presents to this year. You will see there is quite a crowd and from their clothes you can see they are very poor. When the word got around that every child was going to receive a Christmas present, they flocked to the Mission station, asking, 'What is a Christmas present?' They know what Christmas is, but not one of them has ever had, or heard of, a present at Christmas before.

'We lined the children up in two very long queues – they got very excited – and each one came forward to receive their first present; then they went to the back of the second queue to receive their second present. It all took quite a time, but the joy and excitement was wonderful to behold. You have no idea what a delight it was for all of us to see their faces when we gave them a piece of soft white bread and then, when they got to the front of the second queue, they received a boiled sweet. Thank you so very much; your generosity will be spoken of in this district for months to come. With every blessing, Father Hector.'

Table talk

Perhaps we should stop and think about that story for a few moments. We live in such a wealthy country and we are all so very rich, compared with most people who live in our world. How can we learn to appreciate all that we have? How can we help the poor, in developing nations and in our own country? When we meet with other members of God's family at the weekend, can we use the gathering for the Eucharist (meaning 'thanksgiving') to promote concern for those without bread?

God talk

Thank you, thank you, Loving Father,
for all that we have.
May we be truly grateful
and show our gratitude by a real and lasting concern
for those of your people who have so very little.
Amen.

39
Hand up (1)

Table time

One of the traditional elements of Lent, besides making a renewed effort with our prayer and giving up or taking up something, is supporting good causes or, as it used to be called, 'almsgiving'. The people of the developing nations – or Third World countries – are just like us, except they do not have our wonderful opportunities and material comforts. They are people of dignity; they take pride in trying to provide for themselves.

Table tale

These words were written centuries before Christ but remain true today.

If you give a man a fish, he will eat once.
If you teach a man to fish, he will eat for the rest of his life.
If you are thinking a year ahead, plant a tree.
If you are thinking one hundred years ahead, educate the people.
By sowing seed, you will harvest once.
By planting a tree, you will harvest tenfold.
By educating people, you will harvest one hundredfold.
Kuan-tzu

Table talk

Those who are lucky enough to travel to one of the developing nations, where people are so desperately poor, come back and tell us of the sense of dignity of these people. They are not looking for *hand-outs*, 'a fish for a day'; they are looking for a *hand up*. They want us to help them with seeds for the future, with young trees that they can plant, care for and receive fruit from for years to come. In our giving to charity this Lent let's look for ways to give a helping hand, not a hand-out.

God talk

How hard it is, Jesus said,
for the rich to enter the kingdom of heaven.
We are the rich and we do find it hard
to be aware of the problems of the poor
and to share generously.
Help us to listen to your warning
and be loving and generous in helping.
Amen.

40
Hand up (2)

Table time

The last time we spoke of helping the poor of the world with a 'hand up' we touched upon the importance of education. 'By educating people, you will harvest one hundredfold.' That has proved to be the case in Peru, in South America.

Table tale

The speaker in our story is John Medcalf, an English priest who volunteered to work among the very poor of South America. He spent 15 years in Peru.

"The rural libraries started when a young lad, Leonardo Herrera, came knocking at my door. He wanted to see 'books', which he'd never seen before. I said, 'But surely if you read and write you must have seen books.'

'No,' he said, 'we cut a large cactus leaf with a machete every Monday on our way to school and with a nail or a key we carve the letters and numbers on the leaf, to learn.'

Then I showed him a book and he took it and gingerly held it and smelt it. It took him several minutes to work out how it worked. It was a history of Peru and he went away clutching it. I told him that I would lend it to him for two weeks.

That night I thought out how I could set up libraries in the villages of the Andes and get some funding. It was late and I was just dropping off to sleep when there was loud knocking at the door. It was Leonardo back again! He'd come down from his village; he'd finished the book and he was triumphant. 'You can't have read it,' I said. 'You have no electricity.'

'I have read it,' he replied. 'I borrowed some candles from your church!' He'd been up all night reading the book."

The priest concludes: "there are now 600 rural libraries throughout the Andes and it has been calculated that 50,000 poor people use them a year."

Class of '63

Table talk

The questioning of one young lad led a priest to take action that has resulted in a better education for a vast number of people. This is a fine example of giving people a hand up. With better education they are able to help themselves. It is amazing what one person can achieve. Can we stimulate any action for the people of the developing nations this Lent?

God talk

Loving Father,
you want justice and equal treatment for all.
You want us to treat everyone –
rich and poor, old and young,
Christian, Muslim or Jew –
with the same dignity and respect.
May we seize every opportunity to do this.
Amen.

Acknowledgements

The publishers are grateful to the following for permission to reproduce their copyright material:

Egmont Holding Limited, 239 Kensington High Street, London W8 6SA for *The Velveteen Rabbit* by Margery Williams.

Music Sales Ltd, 8/9 Frith Street, London W1D 3JB for *Nellie The Elephant*, words by Ralph Butler, music by Peter Hart © Copyright 1956 Dash Music Company Limited. Used by permission. All Rights Reserved. International Copyright Secured.

The publishers have made every effort to trace the owners of the copyright material in this book and we hope that no copyright has been infringed. Apology is made and pardon sought if the contrary be the case, and a correction will be made in any reprint of this book.

.